FLY GUY PRESENTS:

THE WHITE HOUSE

1600 PENNSYLVANIA AVENUE

Tedd Arnold

Scholastic Inc.

For the inspired and inspiring Glenwood students in
Mrs. Kaminski's 2014–15 First Grade class: Aaron, Aiden, Alana,
Allie, Ava, Bennett, Brina, Callie, Chloe, Cole, Elijah, Elise, Enrique,
Erin, Eviana, Grace, Issac, Ivaliz, Jordan, Kayden, Kelsyn, Marcello,
Mark, Mason, Nathaniel, Noel, Ramirio, Tyler, and Vanessa.

Thank you to AnnMarie Anderson for her expert research skills.
Special thanks to the White House Historical Association.

Photo credits:
Photos ©: cover foreground: Dibrova/Dreamstime; cover background: Vacclav/Thinkstock; back cover: AdamParent/iStockphoto;
4–5: David Sucsy/iStockphoto; 6 top: Poligrafistka/iStockphoto; 6 bottom: Olivier Douliery-Pool/Getty Images; 7 top left: 1000 Words/
Shutterstock, Inc.; 7 top right: Kristoffer Tripplaar/Alamy Images; 7 bottom: Pete Souza/The White House via Flickr; 8 top: Yoichi
Okamoto/LBJ Library; 8 bottom: Annie Leibovitz/The White House via Flickr; 9 left: Underwood & Underwood/Corbis Images; 9 right:
AP Images; 10 top left: EdStock/iStockphoto; 10 top right: Hill Street Studios/Media Bakery; 10 bottom: Bain News Service/Library of
Congress; 11 top: Scholastic Inc.; 11 bottom: Paul J. Richards/Getty Images; 12–13 Washington to Bush portraits: White House Collection/
White House Historical Association; 13 Obama portrait: Pete Souza/The White House via Flickr; 14: Three Lions/Getty Images;
15 top: James Hoban/Library of Congress; 15 bottom: The Granger Collection; 16 top left: Heritage Images/Getty Images; 16 top right:
GraphicaArtis/Getty Images; 16 bottom: traveler1116/iStockphoto; 17 top: White House Historical Association; 17 bottom: The Ohio History
Connection (MSS 114); 18 top: Stock Montage/Getty Images; 18 bottom: Jim Watson/Getty Images; 19: Dirck Halstead/The LIFE Images
Collection/Getty Images; 20 top left: Pete Souza/The White House via Flickr; 20 top right: George Skadding/The LIFE Picture Collection/
Getty Images; 20 bottom: Robert Giroux/Getty Images; 21 top: Marcy Nighswander/AP Images; 21 bottom left: National Park Service;
21 bottom right: Andrew Caballero-Reynolds/Getty Images; 23: Warren K. Leffler/Library of Congress; 24 top left: Dirck Halstead/
The LIFE Images Collection/Getty Images; 24 top right: Richard Nixon Library; 24 bottom: Chip Somodevilla/Getty Images; 25 top:
Jimmy Carter Presidential Library & Museum; 25 bottom: Stanley Tretick/Corbis Images; 26 top left: Courtesy of the George W. Bush
Presidential Library; 26 top right: David Hume Kennerly/WHPO, courtesy Gerald R. Ford Library; 26 bottom left: Chuck Kennedy/The White
House via Flickr; 26 bottom right: Richard Nixon Library/National Archives; 27 top: Frances Benjamin Johnston/Library of Congress;
27 bottom: Robert Knudsen. White House Photographs. John F. Kennedy Presidential Library and Museum, Boston; 28 top: AdamParent/
iStockphoto; 28 bottom left: White House Historical Association; 28 bottom right: Gilbert Stuart/National Gallery of Art; 29 top: Bill
O'Leary/Getty Images; 29 bottom: Mishella/Shutterstock, Inc.; 30 top: Nixon Presidential Library; 30 center left: Francois Lochon/
Gamma-Rapho via Getty Images; 30 center right: Keystone-France/Gamma-Keystone via Getty Images; 30 bottom: Americanspirit/
Dreamstime; 31 background: John F. Kennedy Presidential Library and Museum, Boston; 31: Larry Downing/Reuters.

ISBN 978-0-545-91737-7

12 11 10 9 8 7 6 5 4 3 2 1   16 17 18 19 20

Printed in the U.S.A.   40
First printing, 2016
Book design by Rocco Melillo

A boy had a pet fly named Fly Guy.
Fly Guy could say the boy's name —

Buzz and Fly Guy walked through the gates of the White House.

"Cool!" said Buzz. "This is where the President of the United States lives and works."

Fly Guy did a loop the loop. He was excited!

He zoomed ahead of Buzz and flew inside…

The address of the White House is 1600 Pennsylvania Avenue. It is located in Washington, D.C., the capital of the United States.

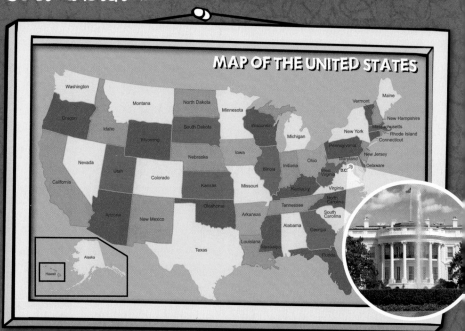

MAP OF THE UNITED STATES

Hundreds of people work at the White House every day.

A WHITE HOUSE MEETING WITH PRESIDENT OBAMA

The Secret Service, the Chief of Staff, the Press Secretary, speechwriters, and several advisers work with the President.

SECRET SERVICE AGENT

PRESS SECRETARY

And a team of chefs, butlers, maids, florists, electricians, and plumbers keep the place running smoothly.

BEEKEEPER

There's even a beekeeper!

The President is the leader of the United States and the head of our government. The President also represents our country around the world and is the leader of the Armed Forces.

PRESIDENT JOHNSON IN VIETNAM

The President's family is called the First Family.

THE OBAMA FAMILY

The President's wife is called the First Lady. She welcomes guests to the White House for ceremonies and special events. If a President is not married, a friend or a relative may act as First Lady.

ELEANOR ROOSEVELT

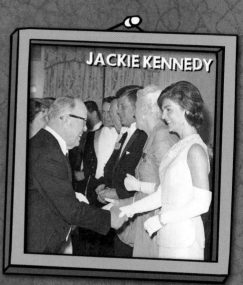

JACKIE KENNEDY

When a woman is elected President, a husband, friend, or relative may fill this role.

FIRZZT LADY?

Every four years, Americans vote in a presidential election. Any American citizen who is 18 or older can vote—including presidential candidates!

voters

Barack Obama casting his vote

William H. Taft casting his vote

A ballot (BAL-uht) is a list of people who want to be President. Voters in each of the 50 states mark a ballot to make their choice.

OFFICE	PRESIDENTIAL ELECTORS FOR PRESIDENT AND VICE PRESIDENT (VOTE FOR ONE)		UNITED STATES SENATE (VOTE FOR ONE)	
DEMOCRATIC	BARACK OBAMA JOE BIDEN	○	KIRSTEN E. GILLIBRAND	○
REPUBLICAN	MITT ROMNEY PAUL RYAN	○	WENDY LONG	○
CONSERVATIVE	MITT ROMNEY PAUL RYAN	○	WENDY LONG	○
WORKING FAMILIES	BARACK OBAMA JOE BIDEN	○	KIRSTEN E. GILLIBRAND	○
INDEPENDENCE			KIRSTEN E. GILLIBRAND	○
GREEN	JILL STEIN CHERI HONKALA	○	COLIA CLARK	○

ballot

The candidate who wins the election moves into the White House with his or her family. The previous President moves out.

Clinton family moving into White House while Bush family moves out

All of the Presidents have had their portraits painted. Many portraits hang in the White House.

GEORGE WASHINGTON
1789-1797

JOHN ADAMS
1797-1801

THOMAS JEFFERSON
1801-1809

JAMES MADISON
1809-1817

JAMES MONROE
1817-1825

JOHN QUINCY ADAMS
1825-1829

ANDREW JACKSON
1829-1837

MARTIN VAN BUREN
1837-1841

WILLIAM H. HARRISON
1841

JOHN TYLER
1841-1845

William H. Harrison was President for only 32 days!

JAMES K. POLK
1845-1849

ZACHARY TAYLOR
1849-1850

MILLARD FILLMORE
1850-1853

FRANKLIN PIERCE
1853-1857

JAMES BUCHANAN
1857-1861

ABRAHAM LINCOLN
1861-1865

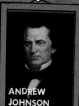

ANDREW JOHNSON
1865-1869

ULYSSES S. GRANT
1869-1877

RUTHERFORD B. HAYES
1877-1881

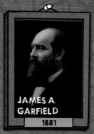

JAMES A. GARFIELD
1881

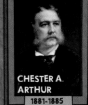

CHESTER A. ARTHUR
1881-1885

GROVER CLEVELAND
1885-1889

BENJAMIN HARRISON
1889-1893

GROVER CLEVELAND
1893-1897

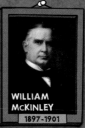

WILLIAM McKINLEY
1897-1901

THEODORE ROOSEVELT
1901-1909

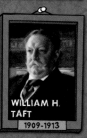

WILLIAM H. TAFT
1909-1913

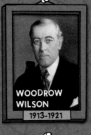

WOODROW WILSON
1913-1921

WARREN G. HARDING
1921-1923

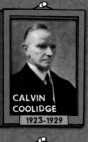

CALVIN COOLIDGE
1923-1929

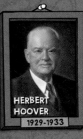

HERBERT HOOVER
1929-1933

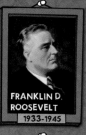

FRANKLIN D. ROOSEVELT
1933-1945

HARRY S. TRUMAN
1945-1953

DWIGHT D. EISENHOWER
1953-1961

JOHN F. KENNEDY
1961-1963

LYNDON B. JOHNSON
1963-1969

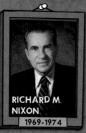

RICHARD M. NIXON
1969-1974

GERALD R. FORD
1974-1977

JIMMY CARTER
1977-1981

RONALD REAGAN
1981-1989

GEORGE H. W. BUSH
1989-1993

WILLIAM J. CLINTON
1993-2001

GEORGE W. BUSH
2001-2009

BARACK OBAMA
2009-2017

2017-

President Washington chose the location of the country's new capital city. It was named in his honor.

PRESIDENT WASHINGTON MAKES A PLAN

George Washington lived in New York City while he was president.

There was a contest to design the President's house. In July 1792, a builder named James Hoban won the contest.

JAMES HOBAN'S DESIGN

WINNER

In 1800, President John Adams and his wife, Abigail, were the first family to move in. They lived there for just five months!

THE WHITE HOUSE IN 1807

In 1814, British soldiers set fire to the White House! First Lady Dolley Madison saved a painting from the burning building. It took three years to rebuild the house.

Dolley Madison saved this painting!

Some people think the White House got its name after the fire. But that is not true.

The White House has always been painted white. It takes 570 gallons of paint to cover the outside of the building, including the East and West Wings.

For years, people simply called it "the white house." President Theodore Roosevelt made the name official in 1901. He even added it to his stationery!

WHITE HOUSE,
WASHINGTON

Personal

November 2, 1904.

My dear Mr. Dunbar:

I am touched that you should have written me from your sick bed. I appreciate the poem. As a token of my regard, will you accept the accompanying two volumes of my speeches?

With best wishes, believe me,

Sincerely yours,

Theodore Roosevelt

When the White House was first built, it was much smaller.

In 1902, President Theodore Roosevelt built an office west of the main house. It was a quiet place for him to work—away from his six children. This new section became known as the West Wing.

PRESIDENT ROOSEVELT AND HIS FAMILY

THE WEST WING

In 1909, President Taft built the first Oval Office.

Today's Oval Office was built in 1934 and is still the President's office. The Oval Office has four exits. Two of the doors are hidden and blend into the walls.

Throughout the year, the White House hosts many special events.

The Easter Egg Roll is the largest event. Children race across the lawn, pushing hard-boiled eggs with spoons!

2009

1953

EGGZZ!

1993

Each November, the President saves one turkey from becoming Thanksgiving dinner! This is called a pardon. The turkey lives the rest of its life on a farm.

PRESIDENT GEORGE H. W. BUSH PARDONING A TURKEY

The President leads two special holiday ceremonies: the lighting of the National Christmas Tree and the lighting of the National Chanukah Menorah.

THE NATIONAL CHRISTMAS TREE

THE NATIONAL CHANUKAH MENORAH

Today, the White House has 132 rooms and 35 bathrooms. There are four floors, a basement, and a subbasement. There are 412 doors, 147 windows, 28 fireplaces, 8 staircases, and 3 elevators.

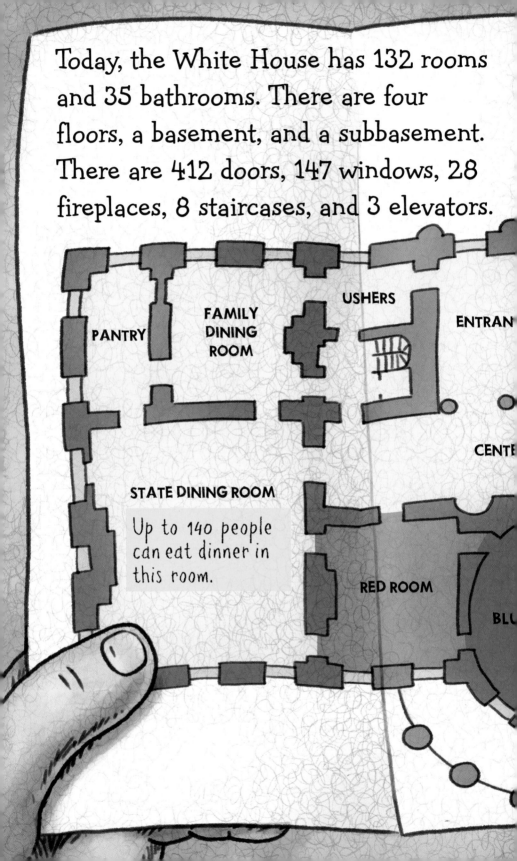

PANTRY

FAMILY DINING ROOM

USHERS

ENTRAN

STATE DINING ROOM

Up to 140 people can eat dinner in this room.

CENT

RED ROOM

BLU

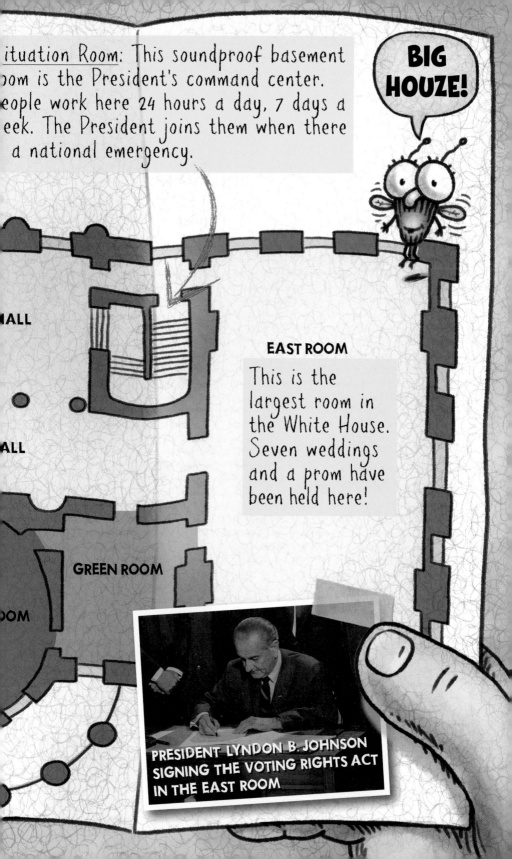

Situation Room: This soundproof basement room is the President's command center. People work here 24 hours a day, 7 days a week. The President joins them when there is a national emergency.

BIG HOUZE!

HALL

HALL

EAST ROOM

This is the largest room in the White House. Seven weddings and a prom have been held here!

GREEN ROOM

ROOM

PRESIDENT LYNDON B. JOHNSON SIGNING THE VOTING RIGHTS ACT IN THE EAST ROOM

The White House isn't just a place to work. The President has fun there, too.

There's a 46-seat movie theater, a bowling alley, a golf putting green, a swimming pool, and a tennis court.

PRESIDENT CLINTON

PRESIDENT NIXON

President Obama painted lines on the tennis court— to use it as a basketball court!

PRESIDENT OBAMA

Many children have lived—and played—in the White House. President Lincoln's son Tad once let two goats pull him around the house!

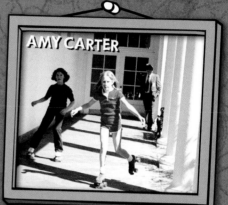
AMY CARTER

President Carter's daughter, Amy, roller-skated at the White House.

And President Kennedy's son, John Jr., often played under his dad's desk.

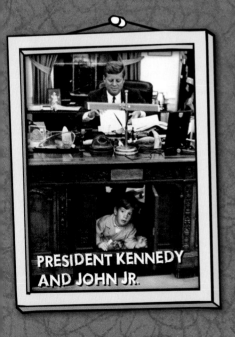
PRESIDENT KENNEDY AND JOHN JR.

There is a secret door in the desk!

Lots of pets have lived in the White House, too. More than one hundred dogs have lived there!

MILLIE

LIBERTY

BO

KING TIMAHOE, VICKY, AND PASHA

The White House has even had alligators! President Hoover's son had two pet alligators that liked to crawl around outdoors. And it has been said that President John Quincy Adams had a houseguest who brought a live alligator to stay at the White House!

President Theodore Roosevelt's kids had a pony, bears, a hyena, a pig, a macaw, cats, dogs, snakes, a badger, kangaroo rats, a flying squirrel, guinea pigs, and more!

ELI YALE

NO PET FLYZZ?

President Kennedy's daughter, Caroline, had a pony named Macaroni.

I guess not.

MACARONI

Some say the President and his or her family aren't the only ones who live at the White House. Ghosts might live there, too!

The ghost of Abigail Adams has been spotted hanging laundry in the East Room. President Taft's staff said they saw her!

Abigail Adams

The most famous ghost is that of President Lincoln. People say that his ghost haunts the second floor and his former bedroom. His ghost knocks on doors and sometimes stands at a window.

the Lincoln Bedroom

A Lincoln Bedroom window

Celebrities visit the White House.

Famous singer
Elvis Presley visited
President Nixon.

1970

1979

Pope John Paul II
was the first Pope
to visit the famous
house.

Queen Elizabeth II
has visited the
White House many
times—beginning
in 1957, when
she made her
first state visit to
America.

1957

2007

President Jefferson opened the White House to visitors. So anyone can tour the President's home—for free!

Even Fly Guy has visited!

"It was such an honor to visit the President's house," Buzz told Fly Guy. "Maybe we'll work there one day!"

Buzz and Fly Guy could not wait for their next field trip.